I am not all that interes~~~ though we need money t~~~ book, while it is about mo~~~ is hardly boring. Jim Newheiser has a wonderful gift for bringing together solid biblical exposition, sound theology, and practical application. This 31-day devotional is not a book on how to invest or how to put your money to work; it is a book about our hearts. Money is a barometer of where our hearts are—Jesus tells us so. And here Jim gives us a book for the heart—a practical book full of Scripture and wisdom. However, I warn you: if you pick it up, you cannot read it casually. These daily devotions, with their biblically penetrating themes and questions for serious reflection and action, need to be discussed. I envision this devotional being used by married couples, by couples who are preparing for marriage, by parents with children, by small discipleship groups, and by Sunday school classes. As a pastor, I will make this book widely available to our church; and I know that it will bear fruit, because God's Word does not return void.

—**Brian Borgman**, Founding Pastor, Grace Community Church, Minden, Nevada

Newheiser provides much-needed biblical wisdom for the ever-present temptations we face from money. Each devotional in this book ends with brief but pointed action steps designed to help us address the sinful issues that arise in our hearts as we wrestle with godly stewardship. Jim lays out a healthy, biblical approach to our possessions. He does this by helping us understand how to utilize our God-given resources for God's glory while also appropriately warning us of the dangers that lurk within our love of money. Dr. Newheiser's words are a timely gift for those who seek to live biblically in a culture that is saturated with the pitfalls of materialism.

—**T. Dale Johnson**, Executive Director, Association of Certified Biblical Counselors; Associate Professor of Biblical Counseling, Midwestern Baptist Theological Seminary

This wonderful book by Jim Newheiser provides Christians with God's money wisdom in the most accessible format I have seen. The format allows believers to assess and diagnose the most crucial aspects of their money attitudes and practices in eminently biblical terms. Beyond that, this book points us all to Christ, through whom lasting heart-based change can come.

—**James C. Petty**, Author, *Step by Step*; Executive Director Emeritus, Children's Jubilee Fund

Jim addresses a very important subject to all of our lives. I would put the topic of finances within the top five issues that people whom I counsel struggle with. Here, Jim walks us through many of God's commands and principles in order to guide us in this area of daily tension in our walk with God. May the daily reading and application of these principles encourage you, as it has me.

—**Stuart W. Scott**, Professor of Biblical Counseling, Graduate Program of The Master's University

Financial stress is a leading cause of discord in marriages and severe anxiety in individuals. This devotional points to solid biblical wisdom that will ground readers who feel tossed about by waves of financial woe.

Scripture says a great deal about money. It gives lots of practical advice on how to earn it and how to use it. But the Bible is also clear that how we relate to money is a spiritual issue. . . . Newheiser offers a steady flow of biblical wisdom to address the complex issue of financial stewardship. While money advice often seems like a few simple steps—work hard, don't spend more than you make, save, and tithe—the Bible reveals that there is much more to it. This devotional does address the practical elements of managing our resources, but it also addresses the heart issues that are intertwined with our views on and use of money.

—**Curtis W. Solomon**, Director, The Biblical Counseling Coalition

M O N E Y

31-DAY DEVOTIONALS FOR LIFE

A Series

DEEPAK REJU
Series Editor

Addictive Habits: Changing for Good, by David R. Dunham
After an Affair: Pursuing Restoration, by Michael Scott Gembola
Anger: Calming Your Heart, by Robert D. Jones
Anxiety: Knowing God's Peace, by Paul Tautges
Assurance: Resting in God's Salvation, by William P. Smith
Contentment: Seeing God's Goodness, by Megan Hill
Doubt: Trusting God's Promises, by Elyse Fitzpatrick
Fearing Others: Putting God First, by Zach Schlegel
Grief: Walking with Jesus, by Bob Kellemen
Money: Seeking God's Wisdom, by Jim Newheiser
Pornography: Fighting for Purity, by Deepak Reju

MONEY

SEEKING
GOD'S
WISDOM

JIM NEWHEISER

PUBLISHING
P.O. BOX 817 • PHILLIPSBURG • NEW JERSEY 08865-0817

Have any feedback on this book?
Write to P&R at editorial@prpbooks.com with your comments.
We'd love to hear from you.

Printed in the United States of America

Library of Congress Cataloging-in-Publication Data

Names: Newheiser, Jim, author.
Title: Money : seeking God's wisdom / Jim Newheiser.
Description: Phillipsburg, New Jersey : P&R Publishing, [2019] | Series: 31-day devotionals for life's problems | Includes bibliographical references. | Summary: "Do you have money trouble? Biblical counselor Jim Newheiser reorients your heart to worship God rather than wealth and presents the wisdom of Scripture on financial and work-related topics"--Provided by publisher.
Identifiers: LCCN 2019021168 | ISBN 9781629954974 (paperback) | ISBN 9781629954998 (mobi) | ISBN 9781629954981 (epub)
Subjects: LCSH: Wealth--Religious aspects--Christianity--Meditations. | Money--Religious aspects--Christianity--Meditations. | Finance, Personal--Religious aspects--Christianity--Meditations.
Classification: LCC BR115.W4 N49 2019 | DDC 241/.68--dc23
LC record available at https://lccn.loc.gov/2019021168

Contents

Tips for Reading This Devotional

EARLY IN OUR marriage, my wife and I lived on the top floor of a town house, in a small one-bedroom apartment. Whenever it rained, leaks in the roof would drip through the ceiling and onto our floors. I remember placing buckets in different parts of the apartment and watching the water slowly drip, one drop at a time. I put large buckets out and thought, *It'll take a while to fill them.* The water built up over time, and often I was surprised at how quickly those buckets filled up, overflowing if I didn't pay close enough attention.

This devotional is just like rain filling up a bucket. It's slow, and it builds over time. Just a few verses every day. Drip. Drip. Drip. Just a few drops of Scripture daily to satiate your parched soul.

We start with Scripture. God's Word is powerful. In fact, it's the most powerful force in the entire universe.[1] It turns the hearts of kings, brings comfort to the lowly, and gives spiritual sight to the blind. It transforms lives and turns them upside down. We know that the Bible is God's very own words, so we read and study it to know God Himself.

Our study of Scripture is practical. Theology should change how we live. It's crucial to connect the Word with your struggles. Often, as you read this devotional, you'll see the word *you* because Jim speaks directly to you, the reader. The readings contain a mixture of reflection questions and practical suggestions. You'll get much more from this experience if you answer the questions and do the practical exercises. Don't skip them. Do them for the sake of your own soul.

Our study of Scripture is worshipful. Money trouble can reveal a lot about what resides in our hearts. The love of money, a race to own the most stuff, unexpected financial uncertainty (such as the stock market tanking), getting caught up in the debt trap, gambling or get-rich-quick schemes, choosing a lavish lifestyle without having adequate income—all of these financial dealings can turn your life upside down. And this doesn't just affect your earthly financial matters—look carefully and you notice that financial distress can hurt your relationship with God, as well, because financial struggles are often worship problems. So what do we do? Do we come up with some plan to rescue ourselves from our troubles, or do we turn to the One who owns all things? The Word points us to Christ, who rescues us from our spiritual plight (sin and death) and reorients our life. The goal of your time in God's Word, first and foremost, should always be worship of Christ. But as we reorient our lives to Him, He helps us to rework the ugly, foolish, or careless parts of our lives—including our finances. He teaches us what it means to deal responsibly, thoughtfully, and wisely with our finances. God's Word has rich wisdom to offer for your financial troubles.

If you find this devotional helpful (and I trust that you will!), reread it in different seasons of your life. Work through it this coming month, and then come back to it a year from now, to remind yourself how to live as a wise steward of your finances.

This devotional is *not* meant to be a comprehensive guide to financial wisdom. Good volumes are already written for that purpose. Buy them and make good use of them. You'll see several resources listed at the end of the book.

That's enough for now. Let's begin.

Deepak Reju

Introduction

IF YOU HAVE picked up this devotional, it's probably because you are in some kind of financial distress and need help knowing what to do and how to deal with it. Have you taken on too much debt? Have you been guilty of impulsive or wasteful spending and now find yourself surrounded by things that you don't need—or even like? Do you sense that your money goes out so fast that there's no point to making a budget or setting financial goals? Have you been caught up in get-rich-quick schemes that have just made your family poorer? Have you been frustrated in your career—unable to find success and fulfillment in your work? Or perhaps you're not in crisis but are tired of constant stress over money and would like to improve your understanding of what God's Word says about your finances.

You need help. Where do you turn? Many voices offer financial advice—some of which are better than others. The loudest voices in our consumeristic culture say, "Buy and enjoy now; pay later" and "He who dies with the most toys wins." In contrast to worldly values, or even your own financial impulses, God's Word offers you the wisdom you need. "Trust in the LORD with all your heart, and do not lean on your own understanding. In all your ways acknowledge him, and he will make straight your paths" (Prov. 3:5–6).

The Bible, which was written thousands of years ago, contains infallible wisdom that has been revealed by God Himself. Some of its principles are echoed by secular experts who, through common grace, warn against excessive debt and encourage people to make and follow a budget. The financial difficulties in which individuals, corporations, and nations find themselves are often due to their failure to follow the timeless wisdom of God.

The wisdom of God's Word goes far deeper, however, than pragmatic ideas for financial success. Scripture refutes the wrong beliefs and attitudes that lie behind financial folly. The most important financial principle in God's Word is that wealth is not the most important thing. Rather, "the fear of the LORD is the beginning of wisdom" (Prov. 9:10). Knowing God and walking with Him is the ultimate experience in life. His wisdom is more valuable than gold and silver. The treasure that He offers His followers endures forever.

Money can be useful, and wise financial principles will help people to enjoy financial success. Christians who hearken to the voice of God's wisdom will work hard, budget, forego extravagance, avoid debt, and save for the future. But their heart motives will be entirely different from those of unbelievers who pursue financial success through similar methods. Believers receive God's wisdom in the context of a covenant relationship with Him. They pursue financial success not merely for personal gain but so that they can glorify God as they earn, spend, save, and give.

Christians also enjoy security that worldly financial wisdom can never offer. Our ultimate hope is not in our vocational skills, our investment acumen, or our savings. For all of these can vanish in a moment, through personal calamity or a widespread economic disaster. Our hope is in God, and we believe that as we seek first His kingdom, He will provide us with the material things that we need so that we can serve and honor Him.

This book is structured as a daily devotional. It seeks, over a period of thirty-one days, to introduce you to the life-transforming financial wisdom of God's Word, through which you can become a wise steward of earthly treasure and enjoy everlasting heavenly riches. We will explore how our sinful attitudes and actions can cause financial distress. We will also see how God deals mercifully with us and, through His Word, offers wisdom that enables us to escape money troubles and to prosper both spiritually and financially. Some chapters have a more devotional emphasis, addressing the heart issues behind our financial struggles. Other chapters will emphasize practical ways for us to apply God's wisdom in our present situations. Even if a day's reading does not apply directly to your circumstances, I encourage you to give it your time and thought—it will all come together to give you a deeper, truer understanding of God's plan for money.

GENERAL WARNINGS
ABOUT MONEY

Money is very dangerous. Perhaps the greatest danger it presents us is that it might turn our affections away from God as we are caught up by the idolatrous love of money.

DAY 1

The Biggest Lie about Money

"Why do you spend your money for that which is not bread, and your labor for that which does not satisfy? Listen diligently to me, and eat what is good, and delight yourselves in rich food." (Isa. 55:2)

HAVE YOU EVER thought, "If we could just afford to own a home of our own, then life would be good" or "How I wish I could drive a new car instead of my old junker"? Have you ever told yourself, when you've felt stressed, "Perhaps if I bought myself that new electronic gadget [or pair of shoes], I would feel better"?

We live in a culture in which people's worth is measured by their financial success. We are told that material things will make us happy. It is easy for Christians to be affected by the spirit of our age.

The Bible teaches that material things can be a blessing from God (see 1 Tim. 4:4). Our problem is that we can take that which is good, such as material blessings or food or sex, and put it ahead of that which is best (God). The biblical term for such distorted priorities is *idolatry* (see Col. 3:5).

In Isaiah 55, the Lord reminds us that idols never satisfy. People devote their lives to gaining material riches without ever finding true happiness and peace. The billionaire Howard Hughes lived out his later years as a fearful recluse. One famous business titan reportedly said, "I have made many millions, but they have brought me no happiness."[1]

My wife and I once lived in a prosperous Middle Eastern country. We watched people accumulate savings, travel the world, and buy expensive jewelry, cars, and houses. But their wealth did not make them happy. Nor did we see many cases in which some-one said, "Now I have enough" (see Eccl. 5:10). As Isaiah says, people pour out their very lives for that which is not bread and their labor for that which does not satisfy.

The answer to materialistic idolatry is learning to find satisfaction in Christ, who is the Bread of Life (see John 6:35). He offers living water that will forever satisfy the thirst of those who drink (see John 7:37–39). And, in contrast to the costly bread of the world that can no more satisfy your soul than sawdust, Jesus offers Himself to you freely. He has paid for the feast by pouring out His life for all who will turn to Him.

Have you turned away from the bankrupt values and idolatry of the world and believed in Jesus, who satisfies our greatest need—forgiveness and restored fellowship with God? Christ died in the place of sinners and has been raised from the dead so that all who trust Him might have new, abundant life. God invites you to abandon the plastic bread of worldly wealth so that you can feast upon the rich spiritual banquet that He offers.

Perhaps you are a believer who has drifted away from Christ and toward the idolatry of worldliness. This may be why you are unsettled. As Augustine said, "You have made us for yourself, O Lord, and our heart is restless until it rests in you."[2] The Lord invites you to return to Him so that your soul can find renewed joy and peace.

Reflect: How have you allowed your financial desires and goals to come ahead of your devotion to Christ?

Reflect: Christ satisfies in a way that none of your materialistic idols can. Will you reject your idols and put your trust in Him?

Act: Pray that God will help you to find your ultimate satisfaction in Him (see Ps. 34:8).

DAY 2

The Love of Money Will Ruin You

For the love of money is a root of all sorts of evil, and some by
longing for it have wandered away from the faith and pierced
themselves with many griefs. (1 Tim. 6:10 NASB)

PERHAPS YOU HAVE heard it said that "money is the root of
every evil." Money itself is not evil; it can be put to good or bad
uses. What matters is how you regard money in your heart. It is
the inward love of money that can destroy you.

Each of the Ten Commandments has been broken because
of the love of money. The first three commandments, regarding
God's priority in our lives, are violated when we put money in
God's place. This amounts to idolatry (as Paul warns us in Col.
3:5). God demands first priority and full allegiance from us, but
the money lover chooses his wealth over the Lord.

The fourth commandment calls us to rest one day in seven.
The person who loves wealth is more concerned with making
more money than with worshiping God on the Lord's Day.

The final six of the Ten Commandments address our duties
to love one another, which we so often violate through our love
of money. The fifth commandment, for us to honor our parents,
is broken when families fight over financial matters, including
inheritances (see Luke 12:13) and loans. The sixth commandment has been broken many times as thieves have literally killed
their victims and people involved in financial disputes have
murdered others with their words (see Matt. 5:21–22). The seventh commandment, against adultery, has been broken by those
who have sold their bodies or trafficked the bodies of others for
financial gain, and by those who have broken the marriage covenant over financial disagreements. The eighth commandment

17

is against theft, which is almost always motivated by a love of wealth. The ninth commandment, against bearing false witness, is violated by those who deceive others for monetary gain. The tenth commandment, against covetousness, is broken when we show an excessive love for money and possessions.

Paul warns that those who want to get rich are plunged into ruin and destruction (see 1 Tim. 6:9). As in the case of the rich young ruler (see Mark 10:17–27), the love of money keeps a person from drawing near to the Lord. Professing Christians have, for the sake of wealth, wandered away from the faith and pierced themselves with many griefs (see 1 Tim. 6:10). Jesus warns that you cannot serve both God and wealth (see Matt. 6:24).

Those who love money suffer other consequences, as they reap what they have sown (see Gal. 6:7–8). The thief, the perjurer, and the adulterer ultimately pay the price. Your sin shall find you out (see Num. 32:23).

These warnings should command our attention. Is the love of money hurting your life and your relationship with the Lord? There can be a fine line between a legitimate desire to acquire more money in order to fulfill our God-given responsibilities and a sinful idolatry of money. Sin is very deceitful. We need to keep watch over ourselves and one other (see Heb. 3:13) so that money doesn't ruin our lives.

Reflect: What kinds of foolish choices have you seen friends make because of their love of money? What harmful consequences have come upon people whom you know because they have idolized wealth?

Act: Consider where you may be most tempted to compromise because of your desire for greater financial security, and seek accountability from a spouse or a close friend.

WHY DO PEOPLE EXPERIENCE FINANCIAL DISTRESS?

People experience financial troubles for various reasons. Some make very foolish financial decisions. Others are victims of circumstances beyond their control. Either way, we can turn to the Lord for wisdom and help.

DAY 3

Financial Distress Is Not Always Your Fault

He said, "Naked I came from my mother's womb, and naked shall I return. The LORD gave, and the LORD has taken away; blessed be the name of the LORD." In all this Job did not sin or charge God with wrong. (Job 1:21–22)

WHEN FINANCIAL CALAMITY strikes, people often wonder if it is some kind of judgment from God. "Did God cause me to lose my job because I skipped my daily morning devotions?" Those around them may suggest that their troubles are the direct result of sin in their lives. "Remember: who that was innocent ever perished? Or where were the upright cut off?" (Job 4:7). False teachers in our day claim that if you have enough faith prosperity is inevitable and that poverty is the consequence of unbelief.

Yet the Scripture says that Job was "blameless, upright, fearing God and turning away from evil" (Job 1:1 NASB). God allowed Satan to take everything away from Job—not because Job was the *worst* of men but rather because he was the *best* of men. The Lord was proving the quality of Job's faith as Job remained faithful even after suffering overwhelming loss (see vv. 20–22).

Job was not aware of the battle that was going on between Satan and the Lord. When we face great trials, including difficulties with our money, we won't be aware of God's secret purposes for our suffering. "The secret things belong to the LORD our God, but the things that are revealed belong to us and to our children forever" (Deut. 29:29). But we can be assured that God is glorified as we respond to our trials wisely and in faith.

There are many cases in which a Christian may suffer financially due to no fault of his or her own. Your employer may unjustly fail to pay you the wages you have earned (see James 5:4). You may be the victim of theft or embezzlement. You may lose your job because of the misconduct of your employer. A friend of mine was fired by a boss who hates Christians.

You may also suffer the general effects of living in a fallen world, such as economic calamity hitting your community through drought, pestilence, war, natural disaster, or a widespread economic downturn or depression. There are many examples in the Bible of God's people being affected by widespread economic famines and disasters (see Gen. 12:10; Ruth 1:1; Acts 11:28–30). Many people come from impoverished homes, where financial wisdom was not practiced and educational opportunities were limited, and are negatively influenced by these family backgrounds.

No matter how wisely you act, you cannot always protect yourself from economic hardship. God does, however, offer you comfort and hope in His Word. He is in control (see Ps. 115:3; Eph. 1:11), as Job acknowledges in Job 2:10. We can also be confident that God has a good purpose for our trials, even if we, like Job, don't presently understand what good He may be doing (see Rom. 8:28). Finally, we are comforted with the knowledge that our earthly losses will one day seem inconsequential compared to the secure heavenly inheritance that we will possess forever (see Matt. 6:20; Rom. 8:18; 1 Peter 1:4–5).

Reflect: How have you and others whom you know suffered financial losses due to no fault of your own? How can your faith help you through your financial trials? How can you respond wisely to difficult circumstances?

Act: Take time to thank God for how He has used your financial losses for your good and His glory.

DAY 4

You May Be to Blame for Some of Your Financial Troubles

Do not be deceived: God is not mocked, for whatever
one sows, that will he also reap. (Gal. 6:7)

SOME OF OUR financial difficulties are due to our own sinful foolishness. We may unwisely take on too much debt and feel that we have dug ourselves into a financial hole from which it is impossible for us to emerge (see Prov. 22:7). Or we may struggle due to failure to equip ourselves for a career through diligence in school or failure to work hard in our vocations (see Prov. 6:1–11). Now that we are in financial difficulty, we may doubt whether we will ever be able to provide adequately for our families. We may even live in fear because we have sinfully acquired money through fraud, theft, or deception (see Prov. 10:2).

God is merciful to those who seek His help. He does not treat us as our many sins deserve (see Ps. 103:10). He has compassion upon His children, for He understands how weak we are (see Ps. 103:13–14). God's Word promises that when we confess our sins, He forgives and cleanses us (see 1 John 1:9). Scripture also teaches us that, after we have made things right with God, we should go to others who have been hurt by our sin and should seek their forgiveness (see Matt. 5:23–24). This could mean seeking forgiveness from those whom we have defrauded and making restoration with them (as Zacchaeus did when he turned to Jesus in Luke 19:8). We should do this even if they are not yet aware of our sin and even if the law does not explicitly require it. We may also need to seek forgiveness from family members who have been affected by our financial irresponsibility and to promise that we will strive, by the strength that God gives us, to fulfill our obligations to them (see Eph. 4:28).

All this may seem very hard, but if what we are describing applies to you and you may indeed be to blame for some of your financial troubles, God's Word gives you hope. Jesus sympathizes with your weakness, and you can draw near to Him with confidence so that you might find mercy and help in your time of need (see Heb. 4:14–16). Satan, who is the accuser of the brethren, tells you that you have failed God too deeply and too often and that therefore there is no hope and no point in calling out to Him. Jesus says, "Come to Me, all who are weary and heavy-laden, and I will give you rest" (Matt. 11:28 NASB). He promises that if you will turn away from your sinful ways, He will have compassion on you and offer you abundant pardon (Isa. 55:6–7). He offers you wisdom in His Word, which, when followed, will provide wonderful help for your financial troubles. And He gives you His Spirit, who enables you to put His wisdom into practice as you learn to serve and love God and others.

> **Reflect:** How have you experienced financial troubles because of your own sin or lack of wisdom?
>
> **Act:** Take time to confess to God your sins in the area of finances and to plead with Him for the mercy and help you so desperately need.

HEART ISSUES FOR THE FINANCIALLY DISTRESSED

Financial troubles are not to be addressed merely through pragmatic principles for success. Rather, the solution begins with our bringing our hearts into subjection to God and His Word.

DAY 5

Who Really Owns Your Stuff?

"The earth is the LORD's and the fulness thereof, the
world and those who dwell therein." (Ps. 24:1)

IMAGINE TWO CHILDREN fighting over which of them can
ride on the swing their father has built for them in the backyard.
The first child is riding on it, when his brother tries to push him
off so that he can have a turn. They push and shove, screaming
at each other, "It's mine!" But their father intervenes to remind
them, "The swing actually belongs to me. I built it for you both
to enjoy."

In the same way, as Christians, we should acknowledge that
in the ultimate sense we don't own anything, because God owns
everything—including us (see Ps. 50:10–12; 1 Cor. 6:20). We
are merely stewards of that which belongs to our heavenly Master.
Scripture also teaches that God enables any financial success that
we may experience (see Deut. 8:18).

This has significant practical implications. It should allow us
to loosen our grip on our possessions. If our material things are
taken away, we should submit to the will of God, who gives and
takes as He pleases. We should also be more conscious of using
that which belongs to Him in ways that will please Him. This
should result in our being more generous toward His work on
earth and more charitable to His children who have need. Our
goal as stewards is not to accumulate the most "toys" on earth
but rather to store up treasure in heaven, so that when we see
our Master, He will say, "Well done, good and faithful servant"
(Matt. 25:21).

Often, our financial troubles result from a lack of careful
stewardship of our God-given resources. If, in our hearts, we see

our possessions as being "ours," we will view our things with a self-centered lens. This will lead to all kinds of heart trouble—pride, greed, selfishness, a love of pleasure, ease, comfort, and self-satisfaction.

Yet if we see all we have as belonging to God, we will feel responsible to Him to be good stewards of what He has given us. If your best friend, whom you love dearly, entrusted you with his or her most cherished possession, would you be *careless* or *careful* with it? I'd hope you would be very careful! And you should be even more so in your relationship with God, who mercifully loved you when you didn't deserve it. Everything you have has been given by Him!

How does viewing God as the owner of all things help you with your finances? Hopefully, it makes you more careful, thoughtful, and responsible, since you are a steward of His stuff—not an owner of it.

Reflect: Be honest. Do you view your possessions as belonging ultimately to God or to you?

Reflect: When were you last quite upset over a financial distress? How can the reality of God's ownership of all things change the way you respond to such trials?

Act: Make a list of all your material resources and pray over them, acknowledging that everything you have belongs to God and asking Him to help you to be a good steward.

DAY 6

Greed for More Yields Less

He who loves money will not be satisfied with money, nor he who loves abundance with its income. This too is vanity. (Eccl. 5:10 NASB)

WHEN I WORKED for an oil company in a wealthy Middle Eastern country, most of my fellow American expatriates were making far more money than they would have back home. Upon arriving, many of them would say, "If we just could get out of debt, then we would be content." After a year or two, they would say, "If we could just afford to buy a house, we would be set." Years later, the same people would say, "If we just could save a nest egg of a couple hundred thousand dollars, we would be secure."

In many cases, however, their efforts to amass wealth proved to be in vain. Married couples endured extended periods of physical separation for the sake of bolstering their family finances, only for one or both spouses to indulge in an affair—often resulting in a divorce, with all its personal and financial costs. In one case, a man who had been working away from his family for four years died just a few days before he was planning to return home and retire. One of my most highly paid colleagues amassed significant wealth, then lost it all through day-trading on the stock market.

Jesus declares, "Beware, and be on your guard against every form of greed; for not even when one has an abundance does his life consist of his possessions" (Luke 12:15 NASB). He tells the parable of a wealthy man whose biggest concern was having enough barn space to store his crops. This man said to himself, "Soul, you have many goods laid up for many years to come; take your ease, eat, drink and be merry" (Luke 12:19 NASB). "But God said to him, 'You fool! This very night your soul is required of you; and now who will own what you have prepared?' So is the

29

man who stores up treasure for himself, and is not rich toward God" (Luke 12:20–21 NASB).

Scripture warns that the person who devotes his life to storing up wealth will never be satisfied with the riches that he accumulates (see Eccl. 5:10). Furthermore, his wealth may be a snare to him that will tempt him to trust in his money rather than in God. The wise man even prays that he will not become so rich that he would deny the Lord (see Prov. 30:7–9).

Greedy individuals often die in unhappy loneliness. Some literally work themselves to death as they neglect their families and their own need for rest. People accumulate so many possessions that their houses won't hold them all; so, instead of building bigger barns, they rent more storage units—the contents of which are often forgotten.

None of this is to say that it is wrong to work hard or save money. What matters is your heart. Are you like the rich fool, who foolishly placed his ultimate security in his wealth and not in the Lord? A wise person may work hard and save for the future so that he can fulfill his God-given responsibilities. He does not let his quest for material things take priority over his love for God and for others. Nor does he put his ultimate trust in that which he has accumulated, because he entrusts his future security to the Lord.

Reflect: Why do greedy people never feel that they have enough?

Reflect: How can you know whether your efforts to work hard and save are greedy or godly?

Act: Take some time to assess your personal financial goals. How much money would it take for you to believe that you have enough?

DAY 7

Christ Enables You to Be Content

*For I have learned to be content in whatever circumstances I am.
I know how to get along with humble means, and I also know
how to live in prosperity; in any and every circumstance I have
learned the secret of being filled and going hungry, both of having
abundance and suffering need. (Phil. 4:11–12 NASB)*

PAUL'S DECLARATION "I can do all things through him who strengthens me" (Phil. 4:13) is often on display at athletic events, implying that Jesus will help you to complete the marathon or win the ball game. But Paul is referring here to something far more difficult than running 26.2 miles. Paul, who wrote these words from prison, declares that Christ empowers him to experience true contentment and satisfaction even when he is experiencing significant material deprivation.

Believers may struggle to be content in difficult financial circumstances. It is hard to be satisfied when your peers enjoy a standard of living that is superior to yours—bigger houses, newer cars, and fancier vacations.

Contentment is especially difficult to maintain when you experience a drop in your material lifestyle. I was deeply humbled when I visited rural India on a ministry trip. I spent a month away from my comfortable, climate-controlled home and slept on a cot in a hot, humid, mosquito-infested hut. The food I was offered was unfamiliar, unpleasant, and often disagreeable to my digestive system. I was intensely miserable, physically and emotionally. It was humbling, however, to see the great joy and contentment of my Indian brothers and sisters, who slept on mats that were placed on the bare ground in the open air and ate much more meager fare than what I was offered.

31

Contentment does not come naturally. Paul tells us that his experience of contentment in all circumstances is something he has learned (see Phil. 4:11) and that this contentment is possible only because of his union with Christ (see v. 13). We are tempted to think that we can be content only if our circumstances improve. But Paul teaches us that we can learn how to be content regardless of our circumstances, as we fix our eyes upon Christ. He was able to move downward from prosperity to humble means and still remain satisfied. Earlier in the same chapter, Paul calls on us to rejoice in the Lord, who never changes—as opposed to our circumstances, which are continually in flux (see v. 4).

What lifestyle would you have to have in order to be content? Paul declares, "If we have food and covering, with these we shall be content" (1 Tim. 6:8 NASB). In contrast to a world that measures people's success by their wealth and possessions, Jesus, the perfect man, lived an extraordinarily simple lifestyle and had virtually no possessions. "Foxes have holes, and birds of the air have nests, but the Son of Man has nowhere to lay his head" (Luke 9:58). Jesus and Paul were content with little in this world because their hope was in the glorious coming kingdom, in which they would be rich with heavenly treasure (see Matt. 6:20).

Reflect: Where do you most struggle with contentment? How can you grow to be more content?

Reflect: Why would those who are prosperous struggle with contentment?

Reflect: Is there ever a time when dissatisfaction with one's present financial state can be a good thing?

Act: Talk to a mature Christian and ask that person how he or she has learned to be content.

DAY 8

It's Hard to Be Poor

Give me neither poverty nor riches; feed me with the food
that is my portion, that I not be full and deny You and say,
"Who is the LORD?" Or that I not be in want and steal, and
profane the name of my God. (Prov. 30:8–9 NASB)

WE HAVE SEEN that poverty may be the result of our sinful or unwise choices or may come because of hard providences in a fallen world. Either way, Scripture acknowledges that life is hard for those who are poor. It is hard to go without the finer things of life and even harder to lack necessities such as adequate food, clothing, and shelter. It is hard for a man who is unemployed to come home empty-handed after a day of searching for work. It is hard for parents to tell their children that they can't afford to buy them designer clothes or enroll them in expensive extracurricular activities.

Scripture warns that poverty may lead to a temptation to steal, which would dishonor God (see Prov. 30:9) and could have severe earthly consequences.

Scripture also acknowledges the fact that poverty may contribute to social isolation. "The poor is hated even by his neighbor, but those who love the rich are many" (Prov. 14:20 NASB). "All the brothers of a poor man hate him; how much more do his friends abandon him! He pursues them with words, but they are gone" (Prov. 19:7 NASB). These proverbs don't approve of shunning the poor, but they describe a harsh reality of life. Perhaps people avoid a poor brother or neighbor because they expect him to ask them for financial help or because they feel guilty about not offering it to him. Or perhaps the poor man is shunned because others realize that they stand to gain little materially from a relationship with him.

The miseries of those who are poor can be compounded by those whose bad theology asserts that God always blesses the faithful with plenty and, thus, that the poor must be out of favor with God. Scripture tells us, however, that God has particular compassion and concern for the poor (see Pss. 69:33; 140:12). It is possible to be both poor and righteous. "Better is the poor who walks in his integrity than he who is crooked though he be rich" (Prov. 28:6 NASB).

God's Word also offers hope to those who are suffering poverty. Cry out to God for help. "He delivers the needy when he calls, the poor and him who has no helper. He has pity on the weak and the needy, and saves the lives of the needy" (Ps. 72:12–13). Even if you feel abandoned and forsaken by employers, family, and your friends, the Lord will hear your cry. This is not a promise of great earthly wealth, but Scripture gives hope that God will meet your needs. "I have been young and now I am old, yet I have not seen the righteous forsaken or his descendants begging bread" (Ps. 37:25 NASB).

Reflect: What is the worst financial crisis you have experienced in your life? How did God deliver you? How can the remembrance of that past deliverance help you right now?

Reflect: To what sins are you especially tempted when you are under intense financial pressure? Are there sins for which you need to repent right now?

Act: Proverbs 30:8–9 reminds us to ask the Lord for the food that is our daily portion—*not too much*, or we may disown God and say, "Who is the Lord?" and *not too little*, or we may feel compelled to steal and therefore to dishonor God's name. Make this your prayer for today.

DAY 9

God Empowers You to Overcome Worry

"Do not be worried about your life, as to what you will eat or what you will drink; nor for your body, as to what you will put on. . . . Look at the birds of the air, that they do not sow, nor reap nor gather into barns, and yet your heavenly Father feeds them. Are you not worth much more than they? And who of you by being worried can add a single hour to his life? . . . You of little faith!" (Matt. 6:25–27, 30 NASB)

WORRY COMES ALL too easily and naturally to most of us, especially as it regards financial matters. You hear a rumor that layoffs are imminent, and you wonder whether you could get a new job at your age. When money is already tight, your daughter needs orthodontic work and your car requires a new transmission. Your credit cards are already near their limit. You can barely afford the payments on your student debt. You want to be a stay-at-home wife and mother, but you worry whether your husband has the skills and motivation to enable your dreams to come true. You have been saving for many years but fear that you will run out of money during retirement.

In today's passage, Jesus addresses the anxieties of His disciples. First, He chides them because their worry is

- *senseless*: As we see how God cares for His lesser creation by giving animals and plants food and covering, we should trust that He will care all the more for us, His beloved children (see Matt. 6:25–26, 28–30).
- *useless*: Worry won't make anything better. No one, by worrying, has added to his life span (see v. 27). In fact, worry takes away from our lives by draining us of time and energy

that we could have devoted to addressing the problems at hand (see v. 34).

- *faithless*: Worry flows from a lack of trust in God (see v. 30). We are not ultimately dependent on others or even on ourselves. God is the one who feeds and clothes His servants.

Then Jesus goes on to offer positive encouragement by telling us how we can overcome worry. "But seek first the kingdom of God and his righteousness, and all these things will be added to you" (v. 33). We are to put off sinful anxiety and instead invest our time and energy into serving God. As we do so, we can trust that He will supply our needs.

There is an old story of a businessman who was asked to represent his monarch in a foreign land. The businessman expressed concern that his company would suffer in his absence. The monarch replied, "If you take care of my business, I will take care of your business." Jesus says the same thing. As you devote yourself to *His* business, He will take care of *your* earthly business. When your life is focused on God's kingdom, you will be able to trust in His provision, and He will give you peace.

Reflect: What are your biggest financial worries at this present time?

Reflect: Is there ever a time when worry or concern is appropriate? (See Matt. 6:34 and 2 Cor. 11:28–29.) How can one distinguish between appropriate and sinful concern?

Act: The disciples had a clear calling from Jesus, which they were to pursue instead of worrying. How could you overcome worry by being more faithful in pursuing the work God has given you? Think of one or two kingdom-oriented things you can do, and ask God to give you the strength to pursue these things—and then wholeheartedly throw yourself into them.

DAY 10

God Uses Financial Trials for Good

*Count it all joy, my brothers, when you meet trials of various kinds,
for you know that the testing of your faith produces steadfastness.
And let steadfastness have its full effect, that you may be perfect
and complete, lacking in nothing. (James 1:2–4)*

WE TYPICALLY HOPE for financial success that will lead to
our comfort and security. Yet God often has very different plans
for our finances. His ultimate goal for us is not that we would have
earthly happiness, comfort, and security but that we would be
more like Jesus.

Take a moment and write down two or three areas in which
you most need to grow spiritually.

Now write down some of the trials you are facing in the areas
of your finances and vocation.

James tells us that we should rejoice when we face various
trials, because God uses our trials to complete that which is lacking in our Christian character. Troubles with employment, debt,
limited income, and/or unexpected bills do not come on believers randomly. Rather, God takes believers through these trials

because He has a good purpose for them. God is likely using the most challenging situations in your life to strengthen you in your areas of greatest weakness.

The person who is prone to pride in his accomplishments may learn humility through unemployment. Those who are prone to self-sufficiency—who trust their income and assets for their future security—will learn to trust God by facing challenging financial needs. Those who lack compassion for others may become more tenderhearted when they suffer economic trials and experience the compassion of God's people during their difficulties. The believer who faces consequences for laziness may learn to work diligently for the glory of God. The family that is buried under a crushing weight of debt may learn to manage their finances more wisely and to appreciate the blessings of having their spiritual debt paid by Christ. Those who lack faith will be encouraged as they experience God's provision.

James reminds us of the responsibilities we have in the midst of our trials. We can "let steadfastness have its full effect" as we cooperate with God's purposes in our suffering. Or we can waste our trials by resisting God's work, questioning His goodness, and trying to circumvent suffering in unbiblical ways.

Can you, by faith, rejoice—not in the pain of your financial trials, but because of the good work God is doing in your life? Can you pray that God will help you to long for holiness more than for earthly wealth and comfort?

Reflect: In what particular ways do you think God is using your present financial trials to grow you spiritually?

Reflect: How are you tempted to *resist* God's work in your life?

Act: Think about how you can *actively cooperate* with what God is doing through your trials. Ask Him to help you to grow spiritually through your financial troubles.

GOD PROVIDES FOR YOUR NEEDS THROUGH YOUR VOCATION

Scripture teaches that God ordinarily meets our financial needs by means of our hard work as we use the abilities He has given us. Because we are fallen people living in a fallen world, though, we may struggle in our vocations.

DAY 11

Work Is Good

The LORD God took the man and put him in the garden
of Eden to work it and keep it. (Gen. 2:15)

DO YOU LOVE your job? Many people view their work as an
unpleasant necessity. It is common for people to dream of the
day they will no longer have to work—either because they have
retired or because of a financial windfall such as an inheritance
or winning the lottery. Scripture, however, teaches that work is
good. God Himself works. The Bible begins with God working
during the days of creation and, at the end of each day, finding
satisfaction in His labor. "God saw everything that he had made,
and behold, it was very good" (Gen. 1:31). Jesus came into the
world to do the work for which the Father sent Him, and He
reminds us that the Father's work extends beyond creation and
continues to this day: "My Father is working until now, and I am
working" (John 5:17).

God wants us to work for His glory. His original design for
the first man and woman, in the garden, was not for them to
experience an everlasting life of ease at a resort. Rather, His perfect plan was for them to work productively in His image as they
subdued the earth (see Gen. 2:15). Later, the fourth of the Ten
Commandments requires not only a day of Sabbath rest but also
six days of labor. "Six days you shall labor, and do all your work"
(Ex. 20:9). The blessed rest is sweet because it follows a week
of hard work. Scripture also teaches that heaven, like the garden,
will be not merely a place of ease but a place where we will work
and serve God (see Rev. 22:3).

Because God created us to be productive in His image, we are
meant to find satisfaction in the results of our labors—not merely

41

in the money that we may earn but also in the good that is done through our vocations. We should be able to look back on a day, a week, a month, a year, and even a career and see what we have done and say that it is good. Experiencing the goodness of work does not necessarily involve making a lot of money. Some people retire from their jobs in the paid workforce and spend their later years working hard as volunteers for their churches or communities or even as foreign missionaries. Diligent students or faithful homemakers may not be paid for their days' labor, but they are working just the same to the glory of God.

Your attitude toward your work will make your financial difficulties either better or worse. Faithful, diligent, timely work not only provides a consistent income but also reflects a heart attitude that knows that (1) God is in charge of everything, including troubled finances; and that (2) once I do what I can to responsibly deal with my finances, I need to entrust the rest to the Lord (Prov. 3:5–6). Which one are you—faithful or irresponsible? Hardworking or lazy?

Reflect: Diligent work brings honor to Christ and meaning to your life.

Reflect: How do you view your job? Do you see your work as a drudgery to be endured? Or do you think of your work as a God-given vocation?

Act: Ask God to help you to see the significance of your work and to find satisfaction in what you produce.

DAY 12

Work Is Hard

And to Adam he said, ". . . Cursed is the ground because of you;
in pain you shall eat of it all the days of your life; thorns and thistles
it shall bring forth for you; and you shall eat the plants of the field.
By the sweat of your face you shall eat bread." (Gen. 3:17–19)

ARE THERE DAYS when you just don't feel like going to work? If God created work to be good, then why is work so hard? The answer is that *the world in which we live is not the world that was meant to be.* The creation itself has been adversely affected by mankind's fall.

For Adam, this meant that it would take a lot more toil to produce crops. Thorns and weeds would infest his fields, choking out the good food he was trying to grow. He would have to fight these intruders with his own hands, pulling the weeds and getting scratched by thorns. And there are setbacks in this fallen world that are even more widespread, such as droughts, floods, crop diseases, and blights. In addition, Adam's own body no longer functioned according to its original design. Injury and disease kept him from maximizing his productivity. Over time his body deteriorated until he could work no more.

And the difficulties of working in a fallen world extend to virtually every vocation. Factory and construction workers labor in dangerous and unpleasant workplaces. Some are injured and disabled. Others die. Engineers and architects make errors in their calculations that lead to the collapse of buildings and bridges. We work among fellow, fallen sinners who may lie, cheat, steal, gossip about us, and play office politics. Bosses mistreat their employees, giving them unreasonable demands and unfair wages (see James 5:4). People are not able to spend time

43

with their families, because they must work long hours and multiple jobs just in order to survive.

Even though work in a fallen world is difficult, God's Word offers us hope. *What is now is not what will always be.* Paul writes, "The sufferings of this present time are not worth comparing with the glory that is to be revealed to us. For the creation waits with eager longing for the revealing of the sons of God. For the creation was subjected to futility, not willingly, but because of him who subjected it, in hope that the creation itself will be set free from its bondage to corruption and obtain the freedom of the glory of the children of God. For we know that the whole creation has been groaning together in the pains of childbirth until now" (Rom. 8:18–22). Every bit of creation is "subject to futility"—it is bound by sin. But one day this creation will be "set free from its bondage to corruption." The chains of sin will be broken at the cross of Christ, where the curse is reversed.

The great Christmas hymn "Joy to the World" also declares this hopeful reality.

> No more let sins and sorrows grow,
> Nor thorns infest the ground;
> He comes to make His blessings flow
> Far as the curse is found.[1]

Reflect: Your financial troubles are due to sin—either your own foolishness or sin's general effect on the world (through tornados, stock market crashes, and so on). How has the curse affected you in your vocation and personal finances?

Act: The next time things go badly in your work, spend time imagining how glorious the renewed creation will be in the new heavens and earth.

DAY 13

Sinful Laziness Impacts Our Work

I passed by the field of a sluggard . . . and behold, it was all overgrown with thorns; the ground was covered with nettles, and its stone wall was broken down. . . . A little sleep, a little slumber, a little folding of the hands to rest, and poverty will come upon you like a robber, and want like an armed man. (Prov. 24:30–31, 33–34)

WHEN WE THINK of our greatest struggles with temptation, we typically think of heinous sins such as lust or anger—but laziness can be a subtle and harmful vice.

The sluggard in Proverbs is a pathetic, almost comical figure who works hard at avoiding work. "Whoever is slothful will not roast his game" (Prov. 12:27). The person who sows laziness will reap difficulty. "The way of a sluggard is like a hedge of thorns" (Prov. 15:19); "A slack hand causes poverty" (Prov. 10:4). The sluggard procrastinates and expects others to provide for his needs. "The sluggard does not plow in the autumn; he will seek at harvest and have nothing" (Prov. 20:4). He is also full of excuses. "The sluggard says, 'There is a lion outside! I shall be killed in the streets!'" (Prov. 22:13). The sluggard shows up late for work, doesn't contribute while he is there, and then leaves early.

Sometimes our laziness manifests itself at home, where we avoid doing our fair share of the chores. A lack of diligence in our domestic affairs can have a negative impact on both our finances and our relationships. One of the most important qualities to seek in a spouse is diligence (see Prov. 31:10–31). Most parents discover that part of the foolishness that is bound up in the hearts of their children is laziness (see Prov. 22:15), which must be combated as we train our children to work wisely.

Are some of your financial troubles due to your own lack of

diligence in your work? Is your present career limited because you did not apply yourself in school to get the training that was necessary in order to maximize your potential? Are you merely doing the minimum to get by in your present job, as opposed to going above and beyond in order to bless your employer and advance your career? Could hard work help you to work your way out of your financial problems?

Are you making the most of your time when you are not at work? While there is a time for rest and recreation, are you wasting excessive time with video games, social media, and other entertainment? What would more effort do for your life? How would it change it?

The gospel gives hope to those who have failed to diligently serve God in their work. When God saves us, He transforms us into new people who putt off the old man and put on the new. Former sluggards who took advantage of others can become givers who diligently serve others. "Let the thief no longer steal, but rather let him labor, doing honest work with his own hands, so that he may have something to share with anyone in need" (Eph. 4:28). Those who were once defined by laziness are created in Christ to do good works to the glory of God (see Eph. 2:10).

> **Reflect:** In what ways, at your work, school, or home, are you tempted to be lazy or to waste time?
>
> **Reflect:** Do you have any regrets about opportunities you have missed due to procrastination or laziness?
>
> **Act:** "So teach us to number our days that we may get a heart of wisdom" (Ps. 90:12). Put this verse into action by making a plan to use your time in the coming week wisely.

DAY 14

Christ Transforms Our Work

Bondservants, obey your earthly masters with fear and trembling, with a sincere heart, as you would Christ, not by the way of eye-service, as people-pleasers, but as bondservants of Christ, doing the will of God from the heart, rendering service with a good will as to the Lord and not to man, knowing that whatever good anyone does, this he will receive back from the Lord, whether he is a bondservant or is free. (Eph. 6:5–8)

WE HAVE BEEN reminded that as we labor in a fallen world, we anticipate spending eternity in a glorious, renewed creation in which our service to God will be an unmixed joy and blessing. One might reply by saying, while the hope of future glory is all well and good, what hope is there in the meantime for those who suffer terribly under harsh and unjust working conditions? The good news is that Christ's coming not only brings us hope of living and working in an unfallen world in the future; it also redeems our present work.

Many of us have worked in difficult circumstances, but few of us can imagine how hard it would be to live as a slave. Yet Paul encouraged slaves to serve wholeheartedly, because their labor was ultimately for the Lord and their faithfulness would be rewarded (see Eph. 6:5–8). The Reformer Martin Luther helped his followers to better understand this principle, as he taught that the Lord wants every believer, not just pastors and missionaries, to see their vocations as service for Christ.

Joseph, the son of Jacob, exemplified this principle. After he was sold as a slave by his brothers, rather than becoming embittered and sullen he worked diligently for his master, Potiphar. The Lord was with Joseph in his labors, and Joseph was entrusted with great responsibility (see Gen. 39:2–4). Later, when he was unjustly imprisoned, the Lord was with him in his work, which he continued to perform faithfully—so faithfully that the master of the jail put him in charge of everything (Gen. 39:21–23). In God's providence, Joseph's faithfulness as a slave and as a prisoner prepared him for service as Pharaoh's prime minister—service through which the people of God were delivered.

We may not always know how our earthly vocational labors fit into God's great plan. Nor did Joseph fully realize what God was doing while he was a slave and a prisoner. Nevertheless, we live with the awareness that *our everyday labor is for the Lord*. We prepare a meal as if He will eat it. We build a building as if He will inhabit it. We do our best—not just if or when the boss will notice, but all the time.

Once I overheard a contractor who was working on my house talk with his partner about how to bury a gas line. To precisely follow the code would require extra materials and time. There wasn't a safety concern, and once the line was buried no one would know. His Christian partner replied, in essence, "God will know, and that's enough for me to do it right." Your honest hard work will be seen by God and rewarded by Him, regardless of whether others notice. "Whatever good anyone does, this he will receive back from the Lord" (Eph. 6:8).

Reflect: No matter your title or job, if you trust in Christ, your labor is for the Lord. How can this fact motivate you to be *honest* and *diligent* in your work?

Act: Theologians speak of living *coram Deo*, or in the presence of God. What could you do this week to help you keep in mind that you are always in the presence of God, even as you work? If it helps, write this phrase on a card and stick it on your desk.

DAY 15

Wisdom's Formula for Vocational Success

Do you see a man skillful in his work? He will stand before kings;
he will not stand before obscure men. (Prov. 22:29)

NOT ONLY DOES Christ give us a new motivation for our vocational labors, but He in whom are all the treasures of wisdom (see Col. 2:3) also teaches us how to enjoy practical success in our labors. Wisdom's formula for vocational success is simple: hard work times skill produces wealth.

In contrast to the lazy sluggard who diligently avoids hard work, the wise worker is like the diligent ant. Without having any chief, officer, or ruler, she prepares her bread in summer and gathers her food in harvest (see Prov. 6:7–8). Wise workers are diligent and productive even when they are unsupervised. Their employer doesn't worry about their not showing up for work or arriving late and leaving early. They take initiative to solve problems and anticipate future needs. Like Jacob, Joseph, and Nehemiah, they contribute to their employers' success. Such work leads to prosperity. "The hand of the diligent makes rich" (Prov. 10:4).

It is not enough, however, to work hard for many hours. Vocational skill is a major factor in determining one's economic success. For example, someone could diligently work fifty hours a week at a minimum-wage job and barely make enough to survive on his own, let alone to provide for a family. But people with vocational skills that are in demand can command a much higher wage for the same number of hours of labor. As today's passage says, they will serve before kings. Employers and customers are happy to pay for their services.

Valuable skills are acquired through education and experience. Doctors, lawyers, and engineers study diligently for many years and are then paid well for the use of their skills. Other workers increase their market value through vocational training and apprenticeships. Skilled mechanics, plumbers, painters, electricians, and other craftsmen also make a very good living. But formal training does not always guarantee vocational success. Some people become highly educated in fields that are not in demand and then struggle financially.

Consider your aptitudes and how God has made you. For example, you may have a natural ability to work with your hands while struggling with theoretical classroom training. If that's the case, you may do best with some kind of vocational training. Or you may find that math comes easily to you; thus some kind of formal education in engineering or business might suit you. God has given you unique strengths. How can you use them to develop needed skills?

Reflect: Is your *hard work* sufficient to meet your needs?

Reflect: Are your *vocational skills* helping you to advance, or are you floundering because they are not in demand?

Act: Are you following God's formula for vocational success? You may be able to work on improving both sides of the equation—working *harder* and working *smarter*. Could you work harder by working more hours or taking on extra jobs? Could you improve your performance on your present job? Do your skills need to be upgraded so that you can earn more for the hours that you work? What natural abilities has God given you that could benefit you vocationally? What additional training or education could you pursue so that your skills could be upgraded and your value in the job marketplace increased?

DAY 16

Looking for Work

And Ruth the Moabite said to Naomi, "Let me go to
the field and glean among the ears of grain after him
in whose sight I shall find favor." (Ruth 2:2)

MY GOOD FRIEND was recently laid off after working for
twenty-five years at the same company. Now, just when his kids
are about to enter college, he has to find a job. What wisdom does
God's Word offer to those who need work?

Few of us have been in as desperate a situation as Naomi and
Ruth found themselves in. They were childless widows in a culture
in which women depended on men for economic survival. Their
situation looked bleak. But God, in His law, had made provision
for the destitute in Israel through the practice of gleaning. During the harvest, reapers were not to go through a field a second
time or gather from the corners of the field, so that the poor could
come behind them and gather enough food to survive (see Lev.
19:9–10; 23:22). This demonstrates God's great wisdom in giving
the needy the opportunity to work for their food.

We can observe two principles from the fact that Ruth goes
out to glean. First, she seeks to relieve her poverty through the
means that God has provided—hard work in gleaning. Second,
she puts her hope in God to provide some field owner who will
show her favor by allowing her to glean so that she and Naomi
will have enough to eat.[1]

You can apply these same principles when you are in need.
First, you should employ the God-ordained means by which you
can provide for yourself and your family. Rather than waiting for
someone to come to you offering a job or charity, you should go
out into the marketplace looking for work. Rather than holding

out for your dream job, you should be willing to do whatever it takes (and is morally permissible) in order to earn a living.[2] The unemployed individual should work hard at seeking work—not merely submitting a couple of job applications online and waiting for a response.

If you don't have a job, your job is to find a job. Your financial troubles won't go away unless you have a job and an income with which you can start dealing with the mess. The exhortation "In the morning sow your seed, and at evening withhold not your hand, for you do not know which will prosper, this or that, or whether both alike will be good" (Eccl. 11:6) applies to those who seek employment. The more seed you sow (or the more job leads you pursue), the more likely it is that your sowing will bear fruit.

Looking for a job can be discouraging. This leads to the second principle we can glean from Ruth. There was no earthly guarantee that her gleaning would be successful. Her hope was that God would provide someone who would show her favor. In Ruth's case, the Lord provided Boaz, who not only was extraordinarily generous but ultimately became a redeemer for Ruth and Naomi. And through his union with Ruth came redemption for Israel and the world. If you, like Ruth, are seeking employment, don't lose heart. Pray that God will provide a Boaz in whose eyes you may find favor.

Reflect: Finding a job (and a stable income) is the *first step* in dealing with your finances. Are you willing to find a job and to work hard? If you are in a job that is neither stable nor providing adequately, will you look for a job that provides better?

Reflect: Will you look to the Lord to provide an employer for you?

Act: Pray and then begin a job search. If you are not sure how, ask a wise Christian friend for advice.

DAY 17

Characteristics of a Wise Worker

Go to the ant, O sluggard; consider her ways, and be wise. (Prov. 6:6)

A WISE WORKER follows the example of the diligent ant (see Prov. 6:6–8). In contrast to the unmotivated sluggard (see Prov. 6:9–11), the ant is constantly in motion. Just as the ant continues to labor "without having any chief, officer, or ruler" (v. 7), the wise worker is diligent even when his boss isn't looking. He works without requiring supervision and doesn't need to be micromanaged. Instead he takes initiative to solve problems without even being asked. When an assigned task has been completed, rather than sitting around waiting for new instructions, the wise worker looks for other productive ways to use his time. And, like the ant, he thinks ahead to the future. "She prepares her bread in summer and gathers her food in harvest" (v. 8).

Wise workers are aware of their own strengths and weaknesses. Some people work well with lots of structure. Others do well with jobs that offer more flexibility and independence. Less structured jobs require workers to be self-motivated. Some people who have jobs that are less structured are easily distracted or fall into the temptation to be lazy and waste time. Believers need to recognize and fight these temptations. We also need to know ourselves. Some people who struggle to work under close supervision thrive in environments where they have more freedom and flexibility. Some who do not do well in a flexible work environment can be very successful in more highly structured jobs.

Wise workers are properly motivated in their vocations. There are many reasons why a Christian should seek to do his best. The person who works hard will be successful in his work (see Prov. 10:4), which will enable him to provide for his needs and to be generous to others. Additionally, faithfulness in the workplace is a witness to the gospel (see 1 Tim. 6:1), as we see in the examples of Joseph, Daniel, and Nehemiah. It is a shameful testimony when a Christian is lazy or does poor work.

Paul also teaches that we should work especially hard for a Christian boss, rather than presuming that we can get by with inferior effort because our boss is a brother or sister. "Those who have believing masters must not be disrespectful on the ground that they are brothers; rather they must serve all the better since those who benefit by their good service are believers and beloved" (1 Tim. 6:2).

The ultimate motivation for working hard, even if we don't receive the earthly reward and recognition we may deserve, is that our work is ultimately for the Lord. "Whatever you do, work heartily, as for the Lord and not for men, knowing that from the Lord you will receive the inheritance as your reward. You are serving the Lord Christ" (Col. 3:23–24).

Reflect: How could you change your work habits to follow the proverbial example of the ant?

Reflect: Do you work best in a highly structured environment, or do you thrive with more freedom and flexibility in your work? Are you in the right kind of job?

Act: Think specifically of something you can you do to glorify God and be a blessing to those you work for in the coming week.

DAY 18

God Blesses Wise Work

A slack hand causes poverty, but the hand of
the diligent makes rich. (Prov. 10:4)

WHEN IT COMES to wealth, people tend to go to one of two
extremes. Some make an idol of riches and are willing to sin in
order to obtain wealth. Scripture warns that God will not bless
the sinful acquisition of wealth. "Treasures gained by wickedness
do not profit" (Prov. 10:2). God judges those who make themselves rich by exploiting or defrauding their workers. "Behold,
the wages of the laborers who mowed your fields, which you kept
back by fraud, are crying out against you, and the cries of the har-
vesters have reached the ears of the Lord of hosts" (James 5:4).

The fact that some people obtain wealth sinfully should not
lead us to the opposite extreme of condemning all who experience material success. People who are in financial hardship can
be tempted to become sinfully envious or judgmental. God often
blesses those who work wisely and well. He blessed many of the
great men of the Old Testament, including Abraham, Isaac, Jacob,
Job, David, and Solomon, with material wealth. He also says that
the virtuous woman works hard and finds satisfaction in making
an honest profit from her labors (see Prov. 31:18).

There are practical blessings to having wealth. "A rich man's
wealth is his strong city" (Prov. 10:15). Just as the ant's supply
of grain from the harvest will help her to survive the winter (see
Prov. 6:8), the wealthy family is able, through their savings, to survive an economic downturn, temporary unemployment, or unexpected major expenses such as car repairs or medical bills. The
wealthy person is also blessed to be able to enjoy more of the good
things that God has created for our enjoyment (see 1 Tim. 4:4).

Wealth also allows us the privilege of being generous to others. When Paul addresses the rich, he does not condemn them for being rich, forbid them from enjoying the fruits of their labors, or tell them to give up all their wealth and live a life of poverty. He does warn them "not to be haughty, nor to set their hopes on the uncertainty of riches, but on God, who richly provides us with everything to enjoy" (1 Tim. 6:17). And he encourages them to use their riches to the glory of God by being generous to those in need (see 1 Tim. 6:18–19).

I once had a conversation with a very successful businessman who was wondering if he should quit his work and go into full-time ministry. While I couldn't tell him what God's plan was for his life, I did point out that some believers can best serve God by using their abilities in business to offer employment to those who need work, to benefit society through what they produce, and, more importantly, to give to the Lord's work. Perhaps He has called you not to be a missionary or a church planter but to work wisely so that you can generously support those whom God has called to vocational ministry.

Realizing this affects how we look at our wealthier brothers and sisters in the church as well. Rather than envying them, we should give thanks to God for how He uses their generosity to further kingdom work.

Reflect: How do some Christians improperly look down on those who are rich?

Reflect: What are the responsibilities of those whom God has blessed with earthly wealth?

Act: I once met a wealthy man who had set the goal of giving away a billion dollars to the Lord's work during his lifetime. What is your goal for using the wealth that God gives you over the course of your life?

DANGERS TO AVOID

For sinners who live in a fallen world, navigating financial issues can be like walking through a minefield. There are many missteps that can cause both economic and spiritual loss. Thankfully, Scripture offers us a map showing where the landmines are so that we can avoid them.

DAY 19

Don't Make Work Your Idol

"Remember the Sabbath day, to keep it holy. Six days you shall labor, and do all your work, but the seventh day is a Sabbath to the LORD *your God. On it you shall not do any work, you, or your son, or your daughter, your male servant, or your female servant, or your livestock, or the sojourner who is within your gates." (Ex. 20:8–10)*

WHILE SOME PEOPLE negatively impact their work through the sin of laziness, many go to the other extreme and become workaholics. When I graduated from university and started my first real job, I anticipated that my Christian work ethic would give me a competitive advantage over my unsaved coworkers. I was surprised, however, to find myself surrounded by people who were willing to work long hours seven days a week in order to get ahead. They sacrificed their families and their health for their careers.[1] Being newly married and also very involved in our church, I found that I was sometimes looked down on because I wanted to get home at a reasonable time at night and took Sundays off.

When God created the world, He established a pattern of work and rest for humankind. The fourth commandment calls us to rest one day in seven and to ensure that those who work for us are able to rest. This rest is a great blessing from God. You don't have to work hard every day in order to survive. God enables us to produce enough in six days to be able to enjoy rest on the seventh.[2]

It takes faith to enjoy God's gift of rest. Many people look at Sunday as being one more day during which money could be made. In your financial distress, you are probably tempted to work seven days a week in order to improve your situation. Your flesh thinks that everything is up to you. But faith looks to God to meet your needs and trusts that He will provide enough even when you don't work every single day.

Christians who have followed this pattern have experienced God's blessing. Businesses that choose to remain closed on Sundays so that the workers can enjoy God's blessings of rest and worship have prospered, in spite of the fact that they give up potential sales on one of the busiest market days of the week. A Christian can skip church on Sunday in order to work, missing out on fellowship and worship,[3] or can choose to focus on rest and worship during the Lord's Day, thereby finding himself refreshed when he resumes his labors on Monday.

The root sin of the workaholic is idolatry. Do you find yourself working so hard that you've made God secondary in your life? Have you turned your finances into an idol? Sadly, as you pursue your idols, you miss out on what matters most. For the believer, all things—including work—are to be done for the glory of God (see 1 Cor. 10:31). As we seek Him first, we trust that He will meet our needs (see Matt. 6:33).

The rest that God offers His people has significance beyond our ordinary pattern of life on earth. Rest, in Scripture, points to the ultimate heavenly rest that we have in Christ (see Heb. 4:1–11). Because of His work we can rest from our works, as we anticipate everlasting rest and peace in His presence.

Reflect: Why does it take faith to rest on the Lord's Day?

Reflect: In what ways might you be tempted to make an idol out of your work?

Act: Think about ways in which you have made your finances an idol. Confess and repent of your idolatry. Ask a mature Christian to help you sort through your idols and to hold you accountable to rest on Sundays.

DAY 20

Don't Fall into the Debt Trap

*The rich rules over the poor, and the borrower is
the slave of the lender. (Prov. 22:7)*

THERE ARE TWO wise ways to address a financial shortfall:
earn more and spend less. We live in a culture, however, that generally looks on debt favorably, since people can buy now and pay
later. Have you used debt as a way to make ends meet?

Scripture repeatedly teaches that debt is to be avoided (see
Rom. 13:8). Under the old covenant, being under debt was an
indication that God had withdrawn His blessing from a nation
(see Deut. 28:44). Individuals who are in debt experience bondage to their creditors and often spend the majority of their
monthly income making payments on what they owe. Because
of high interest rates, they often end up paying far more for items
than they would have if they had paid for them in cash.

Scripture does not teach that debt is always sinful. Rather,
we are told that debt is dangerous and usually unwise. You may
have found yourself in debt because of circumstances that were
beyond your control—for example, medical bills that were not
covered by insurance. You may have prudently used debt to buy a
home, thereby obtaining an affordable mortgage.

Perhaps you have used debt to finance your education. In
some cases, the increased earning power that training enables
may produce income that is more than sufficient to pay off student debt—yet many people incur debt that adversely impacts
their finances for many years.

As many people do, you may have fallen into debt through
unwise actions. Perhaps you failed to live by a budget (plan) and
then used credit cards when your money ran out (see Prov. 21:5).

Rather than being content with what they can afford using the income that God provides them, many people use credit to live beyond their means. Perhaps you incurred debt in large chunks—buying cars, houses, and "toys" that you couldn't afford based on your income. You may have gradually built up your debt with a coffee here and a meal out there. It can seem as though you're getting by—until what should have been a foreseeable major expense (such as a car repair) comes along and puts you in the red.

Scripture warns that one of the most certain paths to financial disaster is for you to make yourself liable for the debt of others (see Prov. 6:1–5). Family members may pressure you to cosign for their car loans or their mortgages. Typically this happens because the bank won't lend them money without a cosigner, because they have bad credit due to their previous financial irresponsibility. The consequences to the cosigner can be dire. "Be not one of those who give pledges, who put up security for debts. If you have nothing with which to pay, why should your bed be taken from under you?" (Prov. 22:26–27).

In the long run, those who rely on debt own less and lower their standards of living. They are often unable to fulfill their obligations to provide for themselves and their families. Sadly, they also find themselves unable to give to the Lord's work. If you are deeply in debt, God's Word offers you hope that through His wisdom and by His grace, you can be freed from debt and enabled to better serve God with the resources that He gives you.

Reflect: Do you have debt? What was the cause of it?

Act: If you have incurred debt due to sin or lack of wisdom, confess this to God and ask Him to help deliver you.

Act: Find a mature Christian and ask him or her to help you come up with a plan to deal with your debts.

DAY 21

Flee from Get-Rich-Quick Schemes

Whoever works his land will have plenty of bread,
but he who follows worthless pursuits will have plenty of poverty.
A faithful man will abound with blessings, but whoever hastens
to be rich will not go unpunished. (Prov. 28:19–20)

WE HAVE ALREADY seen that God's way of building wealth involves your producing goods and services that are of value to others. The harder you work, and the more skill you apply, the more you will earn. Wealth is gradually built up over many years of hard work. Sadly, people try in various ways to circumvent God's wisdom for acquiring wealth. As Ecclesiastes 7:29 warns, "God made man upright, but they have sought out many schemes."

Get-rich-quick schemes appeal to our greed and pride by promising that we can make a lot of money without applying either hard work or great skill.

Many such schemes involve investments in securities or real estate. Advertisements on television and the internet promise that those who attend a seminar or buy a book will learn the secrets that will enable them to make lots of money working part-time flipping (buying and selling) houses with no money down, or day-trading stocks and options from their home computers. Those who promote these schemes typically charge a high price for revealing their "secrets" for wealth and success. These schemes often sound plausible, but on further investigation there is always a catch. Common sense should cause us to realize that what can be learned in a few hours will not enable an untrained person to go into the financial marketplace with relatively little capital and become more successful than investment managers who have top-flight MBA degrees, years of experience, and billions of dollars to manage. "The simple believes everything, but the prudent gives thought to his steps" (Prov. 14:15).

Other get-rich-quick schemes involve various kinds of direct sales or multilevel marketing. I have witnessed multiple cases in which a person without skill or training put himself forward as a financial advisor and brought ruin to his family and friends who made the mistake of following his investment advice. Many direct sales schemes promise wealth for those who build a network of people to sell products that they claim are vastly superior to anything that's available through normal retail channels. While a few people who engage in such schemes are successful, most of them lose money. Some also lose friends.

Are you tempted by get-rich-quick schemes? It is wise for us to examine our hearts. God has revealed His way of building wealth: gradually, through hard work and skill. *Pride* leads us to think that we can circumvent the Lord's wisdom (see Prov. 3:5–6). We may also struggle with *greed*—the impatient desire to quickly gain wealth. In the end, those who reject God's wisdom will suffer the consequences, but we can be confident that as we trust Him and seek to walk in His ways, our needs will be met.

Reflect: What are some get-rich-quick schemes to which you have been exposed? What was wrong with them? Were you tempted to participate?

Reflect: How does *pride* tempt you to circumvent the Lord's wisdom of building wealth gradually through hard work and skill? How does *greed* tempt you to impatiently desire to quickly gain wealth?

Act: Confess your pride and greed, ask the Lord for help, and commit Proverbs 3:5–6 to memory.

DAY 22

What's the Harm of Gambling?

Ill-gotten treasures have no lasting value, but righteousness
delivers from death. (Prov. 10:2 NIV)

MANY PEOPLE DREAM of winning the lottery. In 2016, Americans spent over seventy billion dollars on lotteries alone.[1] Total gambling losses in the United States are estimated at over one hundred forty billion dollars a year.[2] What does this say about the way that many of us view and pursue money?

Only two things can happen when you gamble, and both are bad. You will probably lose—in which case you have been a bad steward of the resources that God has given you. Gambling is addictive. Those who start out planning to lose only a small amount sometimes become compulsive gamblers and lead themselves to financial ruin. People who try to get out of a financial hole through gambling almost always find themselves in a deeper hole.

The other bad thing that can happen is that you could win—in which case you have acquired ill-gotten gains at the expense of other foolish and naive gamblers. The rare person who succeeds at gambling or wins the lottery hasn't worked skillfully to produce a valuable product or service that others appreciate. Instead he has taken the money of others without offering them anything of value in return. It may be that he was lucky. But, even if he wins because he is skilled at poker or other gambling games, he is either cheating others or taking advantage of their naivete.

Some people might say that they don't risk large sums of money but enjoy spending a few dollars on lottery tickets or in a casino. While many would regard this as their Christian liberty, I think that they should think carefully about their involvement in such activities. Gambling harms society by undermining people's

65

work ethic, as they hope to gain wealth apart from skillful labor. Gambling also promotes irrationality. The odds of winning the lottery or a casino jackpot are miniscule. It is often the poor, who can least afford to lose their money, who spend the highest percentage of their income on lotteries and casinos.[3] Gambling is often motivated by greed and may lead to financial ruin. "Those who want to get rich fall into temptation and a trap and into many foolish and harmful desires that plunge people into ruin and destruction. For the love of money is a root of all kinds of evil. Some people, eager for money, have wandered from the faith and pierced themselves with many griefs" (1 Tim. 6:9–10 NIV). Gambling that is motivated by an inordinate love of money is usually accompanied by "all kinds of evil"—including drunkenness, drug abuse, and sexual immorality. Solomon tells us that ill-gotten treasures (such as gambling) have no lasting value and can't prevent a person from death (see Prov. 10:2). It is righteousness that delivers you from death—both the imputed righteousness of Christ, which is of infinite value, and the righteous life that He teaches and enables you to live as you labor for His glory.

Reflect: Many people argue for gambling. How would you answer those who say that the lottery is a good thing because its proceeds help public schools without raising taxes? Many would say that gambling a small amount of money is a matter of Christian liberty. If so, how would one decide whether to exercise this freedom (see Rom. 14:23)?

Reflect: If part of your financial troubles are due to gambling, recognize the foolishness of gambling and turn from it. Don't trust in riches or in rich schemes; rather, trust in the Lord.

Act: What counsel would you give to a family member or friend who is heavily involved in gambling? If this is you, get accountability from a mature Christian friend or pastor.

FINANCIAL WISDOM
FOR YOUR
HEART AND LIFE

God's Word is rich with wisdom that includes practical steps for improving our financial situations and enabling us to live lives of beauty and excellence. We will conclude by exploring how these principles speak directly to the way we regard money in our hearts.

DAY 23

Seek Wise Counsel

Listen to advice and accept instruction, that you may
gain wisdom in the future. (Prov. 19:20)

ARE YOU IN a financial crisis? Do you have debts that you cannot pay? Are you losing heart because you have been out of work for months? Do you keep filling out job applications but receive no calls for interviews? Are you discouraged because, no matter how hard you work, you can't seem to make enough money to make ends meet? It is probably time for you to seek wise counsel.

It can be humbling to admit to someone else that you can't manage your finances on your own and that you need help. It can also be embarrassing to expose the details of your financial mess to a counselor. Take comfort in the fact that we are all sinners who have weaknesses and need help now and then. We have a Savior who invites us to come to Him for help in the midst of our trouble (see Heb. 4:14–16). One way that He provides this help is through wise and loving Christian brothers and sisters. Godly counselors will not be judgmental of you and will acknowledge that they too are sinners who need God's help.

There are at least two qualifications you need to seek in a financial counselor. The most important one is that he or she be *godly and able to help you to take a biblical perspective on the spiritual issues behind your financial problem.* Such a person will help you to repent from the sin issues (greed, laziness, failure to plan, and so on) that may be at the root of your financial troubles. They will also encourage you to pursue righteous and wise solutions to your money woes.

Financial counsel for couples often involves relationship issues between the husband and wife. Has one spouse been extravagant and unwilling to live by a budget? Do they have different attitudes toward debt? Have they been able to communicate with each other in a humble, godly way about their financial troubles? Or have they been avoiding the difficult conversations that must take place? In many cases, biblical peacemaking must take place within the marriage before the financial problems can be successfully addressed.

A second qualification that you need in a counselor is *wisdom with money matters*. There are some very godly people who are not especially gifted with numbers. Financial counseling often involves getting down to the nuts and bolts of making a budget, keeping financial records, and creating a debt-reduction plan. Most churches contain people with a financial background who can offer practical help. Such a person may help you to use software and apps that will enable you to gain control of your finances. You also may benefit from career counseling as you consider your present skill set and training and your prospects for future employment. Christians often network together to help one another find work.

If you know that you need help, don't delay. Financial troubles compound over time. Many people procrastinate and postpone the day of reckoning. By the time they seek help, the situation is desperate—which makes the job of the counselor much harder. You won't regret going sooner rather than later.

Reflect: Seeking help requires humility (see James 4:6). Are you humble enough to ask for help? If not, go to the Lord and ask Him to humble you.

Act: Seek out a godly and financially wise Christian in your church who could offer you the counsel that you need. If you are not sure who that is, call your pastor and ask him who fits these criteria.

DAY 24

Make a Budget

The plans of the diligent lead surely to abundance, but everyone who is hasty comes only to poverty. (Prov. 21:5)

HAVE YOU EVER said, when the money runs out at the end of the month, "I just don't know where all our income goes"? If so, you need a budget. Some may object, saying, "Our finances are so tight that there is no point in making a budget. It all goes out as fast as it comes in." Others complain that budgeting is too difficult and time-consuming.

While I can't absolutely prove that the Bible commands everyone to make and keep a budget, I am convinced that Proverbs 21:5 demonstrates the wisdom of planning one's finances and the consequences of failing to do so. We are to be wise stewards of the resources God entrusts to us. Those who go through life without a plan for their finances often run out of money ("come to poverty"). Some people think that they are doing okay financially—until a big medical bill hits or their car needs a major repair. But these are expenses for which wise people plan (see Prov. 22:3).

A spiritual starting point for making a budget is to acknowledge that we are stewards. One hundred percent of our financial resources are to be used for God's glory (see Col. 3:17).

In many ways, our money is like our time. We have a limited amount of each. While it is easy for us to be wasteful and thus have little to show, we can accomplish a lot through careful planning. In most cases, God has given us enough to accomplish what He has called us to do. It is our responsibility to spend our resources wisely and to live within the means that God has supplied. A budget forces us to restrain our spending in certain areas so that what we spend does not exceed our income.

71

In some cases, making a budget may reveal that changes need to be made. I have sat with couples who are initially unable to balance their budgets. Sometimes it is necessary for them to make lifestyle changes—driving a less expensive car, getting rid of a costly phone or cable plan, or even moving into a smaller home—in order to make ends meet. Sometimes the effort of making a budget forces someone to find a way to increase his income by working more hours or upgrading his skills.

One final piece of practical advice regarding budgeting: budgets are useless unless they are followed. It does no good to make a plan for your money if you don't actually carry it out. In order to keep a budget, you must have some way of keeping records of how much you spend in each category, and you must be committed to stop spending when you reach your budgeted limits. Some people put cash in envelopes for different budget categories. Others successfully use computer programs and apps to keep track of their spending and income.

While budgeting may seem unspiritual, we can honor God as we exercise wise stewardship by carefully planning our expenditures. This will enable us to meet our obligations and to be more generous in the use of our money so that we serve God and help others who are in need. As we make our budgets, we also must remember that while it is wise for us to make plans, the success of our plans rests with the Lord (see Prov. 16:9).

Reflect: Have you tried budgeting in the past but not kept up with it? Why did your past efforts fail? Were you lazy? Irresponsible? Busy and distracted?

Act: Sit down and make a budget using a spreadsheet or an app. Then make a plan to keep track of your finances for the next six months. If needed, ask a mature Christian to hold you accountable to maintain this budget.

DAY 25

Get out of Debt

*Owe no one anything, except to love each other, for the one
who loves another has fulfilled the law. (Rom. 13:8)*

WE HAVE SEEN that debt is to be avoided. Our goal—if at
all possible—is, as Paul states in Romans 13, to "owe no one
anything, except to love each other." What can a person who is
already in debt do in order to get out from underneath what he
or she owes?

First, *repent of any sins that led to your being in debt.* Did you
overspend because you were caught up in the worldly lie that
nicer and newer possessions would make you happy? Did you fail
to make a plan (a budget) for living within your means? Did you
unwisely incur excessive student debt for an education that hasn't
produced income that is sufficient to pay down your loans? Did
you buy a car for which you can't afford the payments? Begin by
confessing any such sins to God and asking for His forgiveness
and help. As you turn away from your sin, allow God's Word to
transform your heart and mind so that you will value His wisdom
more than earthly treasure and possessions. Be prepared to take
positive steps to put His wisdom into practice.

Then, *start taking radical steps to get out of debt.* Make a plan to
pay off your debt as quickly as possible. Lower your expenses by
reducing your lifestyle. Increase your income by working harder
and smarter. If necessary, sell some of your possessions so that
you can get out from underneath the burden of your debt. If you
are weighed down by a house or car payment that is beyond your
means, it may be wise to sell that asset and downsize.

Some people try to avoid paying their debts through various
means, including declaring bankruptcy. While some may be

forced into bankruptcy due to circumstances that are beyond their control, a believer should make every effort to pay his debts, even if it seems possible that he could manipulate the legal system to get out of having to pay. God's Word says, "The wicked borrows but does not pay back" (Ps. 37:21) and "Do not withhold good from those to whom it is due, when it is in your power to do it. Do not say to your neighbor, 'Go, and come again, tomorrow I will give it'—when you have it with you" (Prov. 3:27–28). I have a Christian friend whose business was forced into bankruptcy many years ago, so that all of his debts were legally discharged. Years later, when this friend was again enjoying prosperity, he went back to his creditors and paid back all that he owed them, even though he was under no legal obligation to do so.

It is not wrong, however, to negotiate with those to whom you owe money and to seek a voluntary improvement in terms that would enable you to fulfill your obligation to them. "If you are snared in the words of your mouth . . . then do this, my son, and save yourself, for you have come into the hand of your neighbor: . . . Give your eyes no sleep and your eyelids no slumber; save yourself like a gazelle from the hand of the hunter" (Prov. 6:2–5).

Reflect: If you have debt, what radical steps can you take to get out of it?

Act: Make a list of your present debts, along with a plan (including a timetable) for retiring those debts. Show your plan to a Christian friend who is mature and financially wise, and ask for accountability.

DAY 26

Make Wise Lifestyle Choices

Whoever loves pleasure will be a poor man; he who loves wine and oil will not be rich. (Prov. 21:17)

THERE ARE MANY good reasons to live on less. Some people choose a simple lifestyle out of necessity. They have limited income and must keep their expenses to a minimum in order to balance their budget. Some are facing financial problems—are buried under a mountain of debt and must take radical steps in order to dig themselves out.

Others voluntarily choose a lifestyle of spending much less than they make. Some forego present gratification so that they can save for future needs, such as their children's education or their own retirement. Many believers deliberately downsize their lifestyles so that they can give to the Lord's work and help others.

Lifestyle choices, like other financial issues, are rooted in our hearts. Proverb 21:17 warns that those who love luxury ("wine and oil") will not enjoy financial success—but those who love God above all else will learn to be content. They will find their greatest joy and fulfillment in Him as opposed to in earthly trinkets and experiences. Jesus said, "You cannot serve God and money" (Matt. 6:24). Those who serve money find that it is a cruel taskmaster that offers no true satisfaction. Those who serve and love God find true joy in this life and lay up treasure in heaven (see Matt. 6:19).

As you face your finances, you need to choose an appropriate lifestyle. Are you caught up with money and worldly things, or can you downsize and simplify your life? Our Lord Jesus lived a very simple lifestyle and apparently owned almost nothing (Luke 9:58). He sent His disciples out without money and left them dependent on the generosity of those to whom they preached (see Luke 9:3). Some Christians choose to follow Jesus's example by living on very little. Believers from impoverished developing countries, where a personal bicycle might be seen as a luxury item, could look at the lifestyle of ordinary Western Christians who own their own cars and homes and consider us very wealthy and extravagant.

What should we do? Should we feel guilty for buying a coffee on the way to work, buying new clothes, or living in a spacious home? Should we radically downsize our lives so that we can eliminate our financial problems and then give whatever is left to the Lord's work? In some ways it would be easier if Scripture simply told us *exactly* what to do. But it doesn't—we pray, seek wise counsel, and then take God's Word and apply it to our specific situations. We live in tension. We are free to thankfully enjoy God's blessings (see Phil. 4:12; 1 Tim. 4:4). But we also need to make responsible (and sometimes hard) lifestyle choices that help us to combat our financial difficulties.

Reflect: What adjustments might you need to make to your lifestyle—should you downsize? Simplify? Forgo some typical luxuries that you enjoy? Pass on a vacation this year? What else can you change?

Act: If you are not sure what wise lifestyle choices would look like for you, go back to your godly and financially wise friend and talk it over with him or her. Be radical in implementing some of your choices.

Act: Try to create a habit of consistently giving thanks to God—not only for your food, but for every material blessing you enjoy.

DAY 27

Save for the Future

*Wealth gained hastily will dwindle, but whoever gathers
little by little will increase it. (Prov. 13:11)*

WHILE GET-RICH-QUICK SCHEMES are condemned in
Scripture, God's Word commends the gradual building of wealth
through hard work. A general principle repeated throughout
Proverbs is that while the foolish live only *for the moment*, the
wise prepare *for the future*. Joseph wisely encouraged Pharaoh to
store up grain in Egypt during the years of prosperity so that there
would be enough food for the approaching years of drought and
famine (see Gen. 41). In the same way, we should save during
times of prosperity (our "fat cow" years) so that we can be prepared for hard economic times that are almost sure to come. It is
wise to save for anticipated future expenses such as retirement,
the replacement of aging vehicles, our children's education, and
so on. It is also wise to have savings available for expenses that
we are less able to anticipate, such as being laid off from work,
the effects of a sharp downturn in the economy (a recession or
depression can be the modern-day equivalent of a famine in
Joseph's day), medical bills that are not covered by insurance, or
major home or car repairs. It takes discipline and wise planning
to live on less in the present so that you can regularly put money
away for the future. Savings are ordinarily accumulated "little by
little"—month by month and year by year (Prov. 13:11). They
can provide protection against economic trouble. "A rich man's
wealth is his strong city" (Prov. 10:15).

Again, when it comes to spending money there are different
good options, and we can feel tension between them. How much
may we enjoy? How much should we save? How much should we

give away? There is no simple formula. We need godly wisdom to know what's best for our specific situation.

The Bible also warns that spiritual dangers accompany the accumulation of savings. Those who have stored up earthly wealth can be tempted to trust in their riches rather than in the Lord (see Prov. 30:8–9). Jesus tells the parable of the rich fool, whose sense of security in his barns that were full of grain and goods proved to be his undoing (see Luke 12:13–21). While it is not inherently sinful to store up savings in bank accounts, stock portfolios, and retirement accounts, it is wrong to put your ultimate hope in these things. As you work to straighten out your finances, you should save—but the question is, how much? What is too much or too little? What is wise for you? Begin to pray now for the Lord's wisdom in these things.

Reflect: How much savings is prudent? How much is too much or too little? What do you need to put toward eliminating whatever financial troubles you currently have? At the same time, how much can you save—even if it is a little?

Act: Make a list of categories for which you should save, as well as how much you think you need in each category and what date you should save this amount by. Then make a plan for meeting your savings goals.

DAY 28

Help Those in Need

Whoever is generous to the poor lends to the LORD, and
he will repay him for his deed. (Prov. 19:17)

USUALLY WHEN THE church raises the subject of giving, it
is with reference to supporting the church and other Christian
ministries. Scripture also places a great deal of emphasis on being
generous to those who are in financial need. The Mosaic law
made provision for this through various means, such as gleaning
(see Ex. 23:11; Lev. 19:10; 23:22; Deut. 14:28–29). The law also
included a strong obligation for people to help relatives who were
in need (see Lev. 25:35–38). A major characteristic of the early
church was their care for widows and others who were poor (see
Acts 2:45; 4:32; 6:1–6; Gal. 2:10; James 1:27). A mark of a true
believer is his active desire to help the poor (see Eph. 4:28; 1 John
3:17–18). The major fundraising campaign in the first-century
church was not for the purpose of constructing buildings or sending missionaries but for supporting the church in Judea during a
famine (see Rom. 15:26; 1 Cor. 16:1–3; 2 Cor. 8–9). Believers
willingly made great sacrifices in order to help one another.

Scripture contains guidelines for our giving to those in need.
We have a particular responsibility to help our family members.
Needy widows should be helped by their relatives, if possible,
without the church being involved (see 1 Tim. 5:4, 8). We are
to be especially concerned for our Christian brothers and sisters
who are in need (see Gal. 6:10). Just as the blessing of the old covenant included an expectation that none of God's people would
be destitute, so the church should ensure that the basic needs of
its members are met (see 2 Cor. 8:14–15). The Gentile churches
who gave generously to help the churches in Judea remind us that

we should be concerned not merely for our local church but also for our brothers and sisters around the world.

Paul offers another guideline for helping the poor. He warns that idle busybodies who are unwilling to work hard should not receive help (see 2 Thess. 3:10–11). Some people are unwilling to work and try to take advantage of the generosity of others. Such people are often skilled at manipulating family, friends, and churches. By giving them money, we enable their sinful lifestyle.

There are various means by which you may help those in need. You may choose to give through your church and trust its leaders to wisely distribute the church's resources. This was the common practice of the early church (see Acts 4:34–37). You also may offer help by directly giving money or other resources (such as food, a vehicle, housing, and so on) to those who are in financial trouble. One of the best things you can do for someone in need is to offer them a job or help them to find suitable employment.

Take the example of the Macedonian churches as your guide (see 2 Cor. 8:1–5). The apostle Paul tells us that despite their severe trial (which was probably persecution), their extreme poverty overflowed into rich generosity. They gave with great joy to the other churches. Your financial situation doesn't have to be a barrier to giving.

Reflect: If you have rearranged your life to responsibly deal with your financial troubles, make sure that a part of your plan going forward is giving. What would the Lord have you do in order to help those who are in need? Are there needy people whom you should be helping?

Act: The apostle Paul says that the Macedonians didn't just give generously but also gave of themselves to help. Can you do the same?

DAY 29

Give to the Lord's Work

For the Scripture says, "You shall not muzzle an ox when it treads out the grain," and, "The laborer deserves his wages." (1 Tim. 5:18)

WHILE IT IS important to help those in need, it is also biblical to support those who are engaged in ministry for the Lord. Paul points out that, just as under the old covenant the priests and Levites who served in the Holy Place were to be supported through the tithes of God's people, "in the same way, the Lord commanded that those who proclaim the gospel should get their living by the gospel" (1 Cor. 9:14). To support this, Paul twice references the command not to muzzle the ox when it treads out the grain—meaning that the animal that is laboring for its master should be well fed (see 1 Cor. 9:9; 1 Tim. 5:18). So too we should give generously to the Lord's work so that those who serve us will be well supplied. It also follows that it is appropriate for us to support the logistical needs of our local churches, such as providing them with suitable facilities for ministry.

We also do well to support missions and evangelistic efforts. Paul writes, "How then will they call on him in whom they have not believed? And how are they to believe in him of whom they have never heard? And how are they to hear without someone preaching? And how are they to preach unless they are sent?" (Rom. 10:14–15). It is our privilege, through generous giving, to participate in sending out evangelists, church planters, and missionaries to preach the gospel. Jesus and His disciples received financial support from women who enabled them to carry out their ministry (see Luke 8:3). Paul was grateful to God for the partnership of the churches in Macedonia, who financially supported his missionary work (see Phil. 1:5; 4:10, 14–18).

How much should we give to the Lord's work? It would be simpler if Scripture taught that we should give away ten percent of our income and then could spend the rest however we like. The reality is that all that we have belongs to God and that 100 percent of it is to be used for His glory. While the tithe that was established under the old covenant can be a helpful guideline (see Lev. 27:30; Deut. 12:11; Mal. 3:8–12), we have greater freedom and responsibility under the new covenant. We are to give proportionately to how God has blessed us (see Acts 11:29; 1 Cor. 16:1–2). Giving is to be a priority in our budget—it is to come from our firstfruits (see Prov. 3:9). We should be willing to give sacrificially (see 2 Cor. 8:3, 5; 9:5–6—especially in light of Christ's sacrifice for us (see 2 Cor. 8:9). We also should give cheerfully, because it is a privilege to participate in the Lord's work (see 2 Cor. 9:6–7).

Our giving is an act of faith as we make financial sacrifices out of the belief that our resources will be better deployed in serving the Lord than in enhancing our lifestyle. Giving is a privilege— God could accomplish all things without our money, but He allows us to participate in His work. Giving to the Lord's work also unites His people in love (see 2 Cor. 8:13–15; 9:12–14) and glorifies Him (see 2 Cor. 9:11–15; Heb. 13:16). Ultimately, our faithfulness in giving to the Lord's work will be rewarded, for we are storing up imperishable treasure in heaven (see Matt. 6:20).

Reflect: What place does giving to the Lord's work have in your present budget? As you deal with your financial troubles, have you both planned to deal with your finances and also given to the Lord's work? The two do not need to be mutually exclusive.

Act: Make a specific plan for increasing your giving in the coming year, even if the increase is small because of a difficult financial situation.

DAY 30

Wisdom Is Better Than Money

*How much better to get wisdom than gold! To get understanding
is to be chosen rather than silver. (Prov. 16:16)*

MY OBSERVATION OVER many years of ministry has been
that people invest their time and money in what their hearts
most treasure. As Jesus said, "Where your treasure is, there your
heart will be also" (Matt. 6:21). Many in our materialistic world
place ultimate value on money and on the possessions and experiences it can buy. But Proverbs 16:16 tells us that God's wisdom
is better than earthly treasure. We obtain God's wisdom through
His Word. Scripture also teaches us that Jesus Christ is wisdom
personified, "in whom are hidden all the treasures of wisdom and
knowledge" (Col. 2:3).

So we should pursue Christ and the wisdom of God's Word
the way that unbelievers pursue money. If a prospector is convinced that there is gold in a certain area, he doesn't have to be
prodded to go and search for it. His love for gold motivates him to
get up early and dig hard. In the same way, when we truly believe
that God's Word contains the treasure of wisdom by which our
lives will be enriched, we will gladly find the time to read it. We
will dig deep, through study and meditation, so that we can find
the nuggets of understanding that will enrich our souls.

Proverbs also uses the analogy of wisdom being a lover or the
soul's true bride. "Do not forsake her, and she will keep you; love
her, and she will guard you" (Prov. 4:6). Men or women who are
in love don't merely spend time with their beloved as a matter of
duty. Rather, they will do whatever is necessary to enjoy as much
time as possible with the person with whom they are smitten.

Scripture acknowledges that there are benefits to possessing earthly wealth, including the greater opportunities to enjoy God's earthly gifts that it presents. But these blessings pale in comparison to the spiritual blessings that are gained by the person who chooses to doggedly pursue God's wisdom. As the book of Proverbs lays out, His wisdom enables us to live well—in our vocations, our families, our friendships, our speech, and our every relationship.

While the wealth of a rich man may offer him a greater measure of earthly security, like the walls of a fortified city (see Prov. 18:11), "The name of the LORD is a strong tower; the righteous man runs into it and is safe" (Prov. 18:10). Earthly treasure does not always keep one safe. It can be stolen or lose its value. Or its owner can lose his health or even die. Those who trust in God receive His help in this life and everlasting security in the life to come.

> **Reflect:** How is what you treasure reflected in how you spend your time and your money?
>
> **Reflect:** An eager pursuit of God's wisdom can change your life, enabling you to live well and reorienting your perspective on your financial troubles.
>
> **Act:** What can you change in your schedule and your budget to reflect your faith that God's wisdom is more valuable than silver or gold?

DAY 31

Imitate Christ, Who Paid Your Debt and Made You Rich

For you know the grace of our Lord Jesus Christ, that though
he was rich, yet for your sake he became poor, so that you
by his poverty might become rich. (2 Cor. 8:9)

WE HAVE SEEN from God's Word that it is foolish to take on irresponsible debt (see Prov. 22:7) and that it is most foolish to make yourself liable for the debts of others, since that can lead to your own financial ruin (see Prov. 6:1–5; 22:26–27). Yet Scripture proclaims that we all owed a debt of sin that we could not pay. In the parable of the unmerciful servant, our debt is portrayed as ten thousand talents, which would be billions of dollars in today's money. But even that amount does not adequately portray the extent of our guilt. The enormous debt that we owed could be paid only through a costly death (see Rom. 6:23).

Jesus, who is sinless, willingly left heavenly glory and took on our impoverished human nature. He then took all the guilt of our debt of sin on Himself and died in our place (see 1 Peter 3:18), willingly paying the infinite price in order to satisfy God's justice and thus enabling us to escape the eternity in hell that we deserved to pay. What amazing love, that God the Son should allow our sin to be imputed to Him and then bear the penalty for us.

But His kindness does not end there. In the parable of the unmerciful servant, the master forgave what the servant owed, thus making the servant debt free. This was incredibly gracious. But Christ has done even more for us. Not only did He pay off our debt, but He also makes us rich (see 2 Cor. 8:9). Not only was our guilt imputed to Him, but His perfect righteousness has been imputed to us, so that we may be "found in him, not having a righteousness of [our] own that comes from the law, but that which comes through faith in Christ, the righteousness from God that depends upon faith" (Phil. 3:9). Christ has enriched us so that, when God looks on us, He sees us not merely as being innocent or debt free but as being rich with the perfect righteousness of Christ. As a result, God treats us as if we had perfectly kept His law. In the terms of the parable of the unmerciful servant, it would be as if the master not only forgave the servant's great debt but also adopted him as a son and made him an heir.

The gospel should change how we live. Paul's conclusion is that those of us who have received such grace should imitate Christ by being compassionate and generous. Because He willingly gave up His life for us, we should gladly use our earthly resources to bless our brothers and sisters who are in need.

Reflect: Do you think of yourself as being rich? In what sense are you *spiritually* rich?

Reflect: A gospel-*transformed* life should result in a *sacrificial* life. Don't just be generous with your money; be sacrificial and generous with your *entire life*.

Act: How can you imitate Christ's generosity to you?

Conclusion

AFTER THIRTY-ONE DAYS, you may be still assessing the state of your finances, but we have seen together that God's Word offers wisdom and spiritual riches that are far beyond any earthly treasure. God has a perspective on your troubles.

The apostle Paul reminds us, "All Scripture is breathed out by God and profitable for teaching, for reproof, for correction, and for training in righteousness, that the man of God may be complete, equipped for every good work" (2 Tim. 3:16–17).

God's Word, which was written thousands of years ago, contains wisdom for all people at all times. It's a sure and certain guide for you as you face your financial difficulties. We have seen the way Scripture teaches us how to be financially successful by working hard in our carefully chosen vocations, avoiding the debt trap, seeking wise counsel, avoiding get-rich-quick schemes or gambling, budgeting carefully, saving thoughtfully, and so on.

Have you let the fears and preoccupations of your financial difficulties define your life? Have you let them rule your heart? If so, why not resolve right now to allow God's wisdom, which is found in His Word, to set the agenda for your life?

The Bible teaches us principles that are far more important than mere keys to earthly financial success. We are taught to live for what matters most, so that our lives will count in eternity. We are reminded to put God first in our affections, above material things. We are encouraged with the truth that we can put our trust in Him to take care of us when we are in financial trouble. We are exhorted to live not merely for ourselves but for His glory, as we spend our resources not merely to build our own kingdoms but to invest in His heavenly kingdom by helping those in need and promoting the spread of the gospel.

Acknowledgments

I AM VERY grateful for the patience and help of Deepak Reju and P&R Publishing as they have worked with me on this project.

I am thankful for my wife, Caroline, who exemplifies principles of biblical wisdom through her hard work, her godly frugality, and her generosity.

I also thank God for my parents, who set an example for me by exemplifying so many of the biblical principles of wisdom as they managed their finances, and for their generosity to us.

Notes

Tips for Reading This Devotional

1. See Jonathan Leeman, *Reverberation: How God's Word Brings Light, Freedom, and Action to His People* (Chicago: Moody, 2011), 19.

Day 1: The Biggest Lie about Money

1. Quoted in Nathan Busenitz, "Dollars and Sense," *The Cripplegate* (blog), May 24, 2012, http://thecripplegate.com/dollars-and -sense/.
2. St. Augustine, *Confessions*, bk. 1, chap. 1.

Day 12: Work Is Hard

1. Isaac Watts, "Joy to the World," 1719.

Day 16: Looking for Work

1. Not all Israelites, however, followed God's law. Ruth and Naomi lived in the evil days of the judges, when the people did what was right in their own eyes (see Judges 21:25). A woman who went out into the fields to glean might be turned away by the owner, or the owner might have reaped his field so thoroughly that there would be almost nothing left for the gleaners. Ruth, as a single woman, would have also had cause to be concerned for her safety out in the fields.
2. Gleaning would have been physically exhausting and emotionally frustrating.

Day 19: Don't Make Work Your Idol

1. Both my boss and his own boss were going through divorces, and the top boss died of a heart attack at a relatively young age.
2. God made us to work in this rhythm of work and rest. It is significant that the nations of the world that do not acknowledge the God of the Bible still keep God's creation pattern of seven-day weeks that include a weekly day of rest.

3. It is not unusual for pastors to call church members, only to find out that they have been skipping church in order to work, in the hope of making more money so they can pay off their financial debt.

Day 22: What's the Harm of Gambling?

1. This comes to over three hundred dollars for every adult in states that run lotteries. See Derek Thompson, "Lotteries: America's $70 Billion Shame," *The Atlantic*, May 11, 2015, https://www.theatlantic.com/business/archive/2015/05/lotteries-americas-70-billion-shame/392870/. See also S. Lock, "Sales of State Lotteries in the United States from 2009 to 2016 (in Billion U.S. Dollars)," Statista, last edited August 24, 2018, https://www.statista.com/statistics/215265/sales-of-us-state-and-provincial-lotteries/.

2. See Niall McCarthy, "The Countries with the Biggest Annual Gambling Losses," Statista, September 15, 2015, https://www.statista.com/chart/3793/the-countries-with-the-biggest-annual-gambling-losses/.

3. See Thompson, "Lotteries."

Suggested Resources on Finances

Alcorn, Randy. *Managing God's Money: A Biblical Guide.* Carol Stream, IL: Tyndale, 2011. [A compact resource that covers a broad array of financial issues.]

————. *Money, Possessions, and Eternity.* Rev. and updated ed. Carol Stream, IL: Tyndale House, 2003. [A comprehensive guide to addressing both the spiritual and the practical aspects of finances from a biblical perspective.]

————. *The Treasure Principle: Unlocking the Secret of Joyful Giving.* Rev. ed. Colorado Springs: Multnomah, 2005. [A shorter, more devotional book that focuses on godly stewardship.]

Dayton, Howard. *Your Money Map: A Proven 7-Step Guide to True Financial Freedom.* Chicago: Moody, 2006. [Offers a step-by-step practical guide to getting one's financial house in order from the cofounder of Crown Financial Ministries.]

MacArthur, John. *Whose Money Is It, Anyway?* Nashville: Word Publishing, 2000. [Offers an analysis of biblical texts that address various financial themes.]

Ramsey, Dave. *Financial Peace Revisited.* Revised ed. New York: Viking, 2003. [Offers a specific, comprehensive plan for getting out of debt and accumulating wealth.]

Temple, John. *Family Money Matters: How to Run Your Family Finances to God's Glory.* Carlisle, PA: Day One Publications, 2010. [Offers a biblically based overview of how the Bible addresses various practical financial concerns.]

BIBLICAL
COUNSELING
COALITION

The Biblical Counseling Coalition (BCC) is passionate about enhancing and advancing biblical counseling globally. We accomplish this through broadcasting, connecting, and collaborating.

Broadcasting promotes gospel-centered biblical counseling ministries and resources to bring hope and healing to hurting people around the world. We promote biblical counseling in a number of ways: through our *15:14* podcast, website (biblicalcounselingcoalition.org), partner ministry, conference attendance, and personal relationships.

Connecting biblical counselors and biblical counseling ministries is a central component of the BCC. The BCC was founded by leaders in the biblical counseling movement who saw the need for and the power behind building a strong global network of biblical counselors. We introduce individuals and ministries to one another to establish gospel-centered relationships.

Collaboration is the natural outgrowth of our connecting efforts. We truly believe that biblical counselors and ministries can accomplish more by working together. The BCC Confessional Statement, which is a clear and comprehensive definition of biblical counseling, was created through the cooperative effort of over thirty leading biblical counselors. The BCC has also published a three-part series of multi-contributor works that bring theological wisdom and practical expertise to pastors, church leaders, counseling practitioners, and students. Each year we are able to facilitate the production of numerous resources, including books, articles, videos, audio resources, and a host of other helps for biblical counselors. Working together allows us to provide robust resources and develop best practices in biblical counseling so that we can hone the ministry of soul care in the church.

To learn more about the BCC, visit biblicalcounselingcoalition.org.